When Wilding Returns

Carol Lee Saffioti-Hughes

Cyberwit.net
HIG 45 Kaushambi Kunj, Kalindipuram
Allahabad - 211011 (U.P.) India
http://www.cyberwit.net
Tel: +(91) 9415091004
E-mail: info@cyberwit.net

Printed at Replika Press.

*This collection is dedicated to my husband Ted
and my daughter, Autumn Grace: "I carry you"...*

Contents

The Mothers

Rachel wept unceasing
for her children were no more

Rubens' mothers struggled
yet fought back
arms muscular and desperate
tearing at the faces...
slaughter of the innocents.

Would mothers who had no chance
to confront the attacker
envy those women
a chance to die for their children
a luxury
the ruthlessness of the killer
not granting?

A blood tornado
sweeping little Bethlehem
repeated in so many towns—
Columbine, Sandy Hook,
Uvalde—
a litany of teddy bears
hover near a pool of light.

19 voices sing no more
their desperate cries
hollow echoing

cry for help
from men who failed them.

A shiver passes over me
I grab for air
as I know
if the mothers had been
the other side of the door
they would have taken the guns
from stunned men
and raged, raged, into that day.

Time, Tide, and Stars

Circling galaxies
some swirl left, others right
in the illusion of a single plane
children's pinwheels
freed from their sticks
whirling past other star clouds
as the waves wash in
over stone, sand, smooth glass.

The water rises, the water falls
gathers to centers
catches facets of sun
as sand becomes stars.

I sense one moment
 fall into light shards
wave crest gathers
stillness
then a rushing back from the shore.

Shore and water, water and stone
tide and moon
moon and stars
rise.

The Bonsai Master

Please do not touch the Bonsai.
Alarm will sound—
You will not hear it
but he will know.
It's a matter of synergy
between a plant and its shaper.

He spends time
in the garden
waiting for the moment
to make one single cut
but he will rise from his reverie

for he is there all seasons
pouring the secrets of hidden worlds
through his thinning fingers
when he is pruning.

The Bonsai will tremble
you will not see it
but the vibration
will set him to pause
just for an instant
and he will turn
to comfort the Bonsai
knowing
you have disturbed the universe.

On Being Two Places At Once

This man Luis Alberto Urrea
spoke last night of his life—
liminal spaces—he said.

The torture:
blood of oppressed
and oppressor in his veins
born of mixed origins
crossing borders of his youth
turned to many years seeking
the stories inflamed.
Both sides of a dark border.

He found he could write
of those who die in the desert
seeking the dreams of the north
while also encountering
 a border patrolman
who goes out with water
searching—
brings the desperate ones
stateside
only to arrest them.

But Luis could not hate
this particular arm of the law
for saving a life.
Perhaps better to capture a wanderer

than send home a body bag—
liminal spaces.

As I ponder words that assure me
every line carves two sides—
slashes part the flesh
I think of my Italian American father
once a border patrolman.

They thought he could speak Spanish
sent him to Texas
he told them he could not
and I wonder
what he did there
in that same desert.
I wonder because
I still have his gun.

Starlight Through Amberwood

In the October night
pinewood breathing in the air
an iron burning circle on the ground.
Wine to warm
flame to fire our faces
breath cold
air at our backs.

There are no stars you said
and the flames began to melt
rain up
the color of amber
warm hardsoft touchable to palms
pinewood flames to gold.

Stars, of course, for there were
no clouds in that night
but the glow of amberwood light
throwing off the rest
and chip sparks
flecked the air flying up
lighting the lines of your face
tree shadows from the near horizon.

There were no stars
but amberlight.

Spirit Smoke

These are the days when the starlings hover
clustering shelter in early dusklight
windways in leaf places grow more urging
insist on listenways, the earth turns ear.

Longer the sun rays greener than gold
tasseled corn cobbles in fields not yet bent.
Pressing the ground, seeds balloon, sides burst—
set, not rising, spirit smoke lingers
not yet the frost whip wind in the night.

Deer Woman

Eyes glazed
reflecting lights around her
I see her in my dream
her hide winter-darkened
legs unsteady on concrete
she darts
ears twitching
hears the hunter
in the stillness of the desert.

She morphs
with my stirring
from Erdrich's antelope wife
to Kahlo's little deer
pines surround her
antlers rising
those black coiled braids
her head lowers
tail raises, about to flag.

I reach out
she draws back
ready to break
flank scored by arrows
pawing the tarmac
as if it will yield to her hoof.

In cityscape or darkening forest
she is there

sister image
running.
Night hunter
pursues with jacklights.

The Field Rises, The Field Falls

I've walked this path
in daylight and dreams
mid-summer when the St. John's Wort
blends the field in yellow and ochre.
Later in purple when the bee balm
 nods, holding bold
against the invading Knapweed.
We pull so much we bloody our hands.
The fragrant Lead Plant at edges of sun
yields a rising smell of a mint-like green.

 We bought the land knowing
it is the Menominee
whose ground we walk
lost in the ceding to logging barons.
The People of the Wild Rice knew
land can never be bought or sold.
First white settler cabin
 failing into the hillside
stone silo still standing.
The owner before us
stripped it to sell off
and we, not knowing,
 found it later
barren of live things.
Trusting,
we had walked the land in fall,
 bought in winter.

So we coax, enrich in hope.
I scatter native seed
after first snow each year
and dream through the winter,
seeds drifting slowly to ground.

The field breathes with the wind
like the flanks of the deer
who bed down in tall Blue Stem.
Along the path we cut
Black Eyes grow wild—
we never planted, we just watch in wonder.
The pie-eyed daisies seem
to like the sandy soil.
We leave them nodding
to each other
though they are intruders.

At least the land holds enough
to spread the milkweed
as we go seeking chrysalis signs.
It's not been so good a year—
haven't seen too many Monarchs

The turkeys—
with their jakes and jennies—
favor dusting in the sand back of the field.
Gifts, sometimes down belly feathers
or long silken tail feathers
I put in blue and brown medicine bottles
recovered by farmyard archaeology.

I keep notes on each passing year.
Mind you, winters can be harsh
but that's another story.
We've become good trackers
of scat and paw prints.

Trapped

I walked into her life
when she was trapped
in a madness:
fluorescence and concrete
high pitched calls
somehow pinging only me.

Things flying through the air
from an audience
books, jacket, soda cups
the crowd collectively
whipping up their Grimm dreams
into a bad black-and-white flick.
Stoker and Lugosi conjured
maestros in the cacophony
but she was ailing
striking glass and stone
spiraling down the staircase
surrendering hopes of escape.
I said her name:
Fingerwing.

I told everyone
Leave.
My arm lifted puppet-like
pulled by some shared sense
of ancient anatomy of flight
her finger-like wings beckoning.
I hoped outrageously that she would

sense my hand.
No flailing formation
of many wings, no colony in the dark
just two outstretched
wings.

I walked the stone floor
arm raised, my hand wide spread
letting her wingbeat and breathing
calm to mine.
Air could no longer lift her.
She fell.

Not looking back
I heard
desperate scrabbling behind me.
Ground-bound she bore no magic
more vulnerable than a mouse.

Still, she followed.
We reached
the glass walls that bound her.

Her mouth opened, failing
as she scratched at the floor
to the open door.
Out she crept as I held it for her
under the sidewalk lamp
she enfolded all her force.
And then
she flew.

Plein Air

The skyline hints of a second glass of wine
when anywhere goes and the sun drops low
the pines straight—pencils against the sky
with brushstroke branches—a haiku hand
defines there by the gone, near by the hear
wing beats strike across the lowering light
as the small light slips, the pale blue greys
pass the curtain's sheer glow, still seep
into the jagged between the house shadows
and the sumac trees brush,
content to bend to the ground.

Prayer Flag

for Cheryl Mahowald's weaving, "Prayer Flag"

Bless the tree yielding the branch
 that holds
the fine strands and fibers, found glass
other thoughtful bits of simple things.

Bless the strands interwoven
nudging
each other into meaning
threads fall downward to earth
rise upward to sky.

Bless the yarn that yields a piece of itself
to the weaver
threads, re-threads
to make of many parts this shimmering whole

Bless the hands of the weaver pausing
in rhythm with earth beneath her feet
murmurations of air to make the pieces breathe

Bless the eye of the weaver
seeing
in simple small things
a shard, a fleck, a tumble of threads
vision that strangers might otherwise miss.

Bless the whispers of the weaver
speaking to her work
selecting time
when to bind, what to unbind, when to cut
strands become knots
this binding of self and soul
that otherwise would not be.

Bless the receivers of all these gifts—
crowds erupting
a lone child crossing a fierce border
waiting with a bowl nothing at all
like the nourishment of homeland
father left behind to fight
mother hovering, her heartsblood spent—
with this woven oneness
we can hear their tears.

Putting It Off

House of few rooms
century old four-square
kitchen added later
chairs face each other to make a shelf
clothes won't fit in the corner dresser
black stripes on a red wool trade blanket
slung over a chair back .

Pedestal fan in the front of the window
whether we need it or not.
Piles of loose poems, chapbooks and journals on the floor
books squeezed between my chair and lamp
shoes tucked under the recliner on his side.

Kitchen table half desk and work space, never clear.
A cracked crockery mixing bowl, bought at a flea market
thick and thin blue lines round the rim
holds summer fruits and a stray envelope.
Towels rolled next to books.

More collected things on the porches:
a telescope, a Good Will boom box for listening to games,
my brother-in-law's ashes in a brown plastic box:
some scattered on the lake
some on his land
some still in that box.

Remembering Naomi Nye's "Burning the Old Year"

At a church I used to attend
a watcher invited all:
write the worst of the passing year
on a slip of paper
as if only one argument
one jealous ending
one forgotten appointment
in the year.
Perhaps some of us still knew shorthand.

We walked to the front
it wasn't called an altar
we were all in the whirl together
no sacred separation
between those who spoke
and those who listened.
Yet I hesitated.

Her poem was in my head—
"so much of any year is flammable."

The ritual required
a burning bowl
and so we dropped
missed lines and cues
the whole past year.
Flames and cinders spiral up
to the wooden beams

along the stained windows—
some prairie school abstract design,
but a christ among them.
Along the ceiling words failed.

"Shuffle of losses and leaves"—
breaking like shards of glass
unfinished letters
leaving ashes in the bowl—
the watchers burning the past.

This Is Your Poem, Rabbit

I remember asking you
was it a coyote
but I knew
he would have taken you with him.
I came closer
you couldn't run
I nudged you
there was no blood
your ears laid back
and I stroked that soft inner space
between my fingers.

I never thought
the wildness in you
would ever let me hold you
but there we sat a while
you in my lap
I felt the length of you
no breaks
and no leaping away in pain.

It was early spring
I remember a racing under your ribs
your chest rising in quick half breaths
the shed door swinging
in the March wind.

Did you get in there
find something,
as I pondered

the rage of every argument
unresolved in the house
stuff to kill still in the shed?

Your eyes opened
as if to see if I was still there
and mine closed
as if shutting out the world
could make it go away
or help you stay in it.

When Wilding Returns

Crossing a field no longer farmed
purple asters huddle in clusters
against this sky slanted in orange waves
the rays dapple yellow sunbonnets
tawny sweetgrass, red-tipped prairie grass,
Brown-eyed Susans,
small bursts of chamomile
ready for tea.
Splayed hoof prints in ochre sand
say the doe and her fawns
still forage together.
When fall's flames
dim, early winter will bring
the grey buck, the hunter close behind.

Oh to be a princess

Her kingdom a chessboard
her subjects the ducklings at her feet
her tiara a bit askew
her black regalia
casual,
no fluff or tulle.

Legs adorned with striped red and white socks
her favorite shoes
no heels
no smiles for the beholder
relaxed in her favorite black chair
her gaze beyond us
contemplating her own universe.

When a Raven Dies

Others swarm
circle in
dark wings in a darkening sky
portents some say.

I have no fear of them
for my native name is Raven
Ka-Ga-Shi
in Potawatomi I am told—
from the world
we humans rarely touch.

The children nearby
 are day and night:
dead raven at their feet
white raven on a tree stump
a message bearer.

I will wake knowing
I have been visited
and a day from a dream will follow.

Findings

I unpack boxes of pictures
my mother left:
photos of the ship crossings
to Scotland, my grandfather's homeland,
a banana-curl child
pushing a china doll
in a wicker pram,
thirties era car
and a smiling couple.

40's era:
three young women
in prim dresses
sitting on a rock
but showing a little leg.

Falling from an envelope
the V mail from my father
during WW II sent from along
the Burma Lido road.
I turn a picture of my dad
and find his message:
the mountains round
remind me of your breasts.
A statue of the Buddha
the platoon stumbled upon
rises from the stones.

On Rising

Cigarette smoke rises from a saucer
stray things on the wall
faded newspaper clippings
red paint splatter weeps
into a calendar of too many days x'd.
my eyes stray to a water-streaked window
frost birches haunt me
I find a thrush perched on a branch—
is it out there or on the wall?
broken telescope on the porch
I can only look inward now
who are the men shadowed in the clipping?
letters splattered across a page
what word
does the red letter T portend?

Neighbors

Most times standing at the kitchen door
coffee in hand, I pause
before entering the day
take a breath
peer out the green-framed window.

I know to check for live things:
I surprise rabbits that chew
the porch boards in winter,
or my sunflowers when the sprouts are new.
Deer will dart from eating my early roses.

I notice I left the garbage lid off.
Occasional black bear might show—
our only kind in these parts.
At least, no scattered scraps.
folks tell us
we are fools to leave cans out.

So far, a bear has appeared only once.
A yearling, we could tell—
less than two hundred pounds—
didn't knock over the bins
just passed through, broad daylight.
Never touched the bird feeders
which in summer we also know
we shouldn't fill.
We built a locker for the garbage.
but the feeders stay.

The coffee tepids by the time I unlock the door.
We at least lock now, mostly for their sake—
bears can learn to turn a handle.
I will finally venture out
looking for scat
rumpling in the flower beds
or tracks in snow.
There are worse habits.

Tracks

Not much goes to waste up here
50 rows of corn
more than we can use—
 wild rabbits, voles, birds, deer get their share.
The voles sometimes go to the barn owl—
the rabbits, to the hawks.
some of the rabbits, just too young to know:
don't go sunning out from under the pines too far—
leap too late from those shadows overhead
and dark on snow will be the last thing you see.
 The tracks change with the weather
first young of a rabbit year—
even they can do a three foot leap
in clean snow. We have seen them
in the mid-day sun.

Scraps from the meal
wind up in the coyote hang-out—
we try to help them along
hoping they will leave the chickens alone
but we know nightfall
brings the round-up calls.
most people can't tell a coyote from a fox
on the horizon
but you learn.

Sometimes we notice matted blood
not much left, not even many feathers
when the single digit nights sink in.

As for pine squirrels?
let's just say —
there is a difference of opinion
in the household.
One of us says
they're just more mouths to feed.
The other? Well, the rifle
standing in the back hall
is there for a reason:

Was it Hemingway who said
if a gun shows up in a story
it has to go off?

Day of the Dead

Sunlight at dusk
brushstrokes from tree limbs
cross the sky
no flaming leaves
to soften the horizon
wind gathers
from empty trees on the hillside
whips down the back sand trail
from the corner of the barn.

I walk this time of year
to breathe an air once full of gold
now ochre and grey
as smoke from burning leaf piles rises.

A smudging—
I turn in to the smoke, as long as I can
to let it rise over me, into me
let me fall with that fall
let me rise with that smoke
a ghost meal ready
a spirit guides me through this day's longing.

From Where I Stand

First glimpse came late
their echoing honks
so long in the sky
when searching the clouds and grey
revealed nothing
I doubted them.

Yet they insisted their way
through a lowering dusk
streamed overhead
like water rushing by,
all sound, no color
but the changing rays against clouds
gradually revealing
overlapping V's
dropping in the air enough
I could see faint outlines
match their haunting calls.

How do they fly without the things
we need for flight?
Their calls become sonar and radar,
they reckon altitude, speed—
pace themselves as they lower
changing formations
gently morphing
one shape into another—
haunting, haunting the air with their voices.

They circle, gather, drop
on water to be safe
from shoreline threats
and still I stand
caught by their joining of sound and night.

Homage to Anna Seward

An Evening in November, 1754

The rain is stopped, but heavy drops still fall.
From the drenched roof, and dark wind
Rounds dim hills. Still over hard passages
Winds whine through jagged rocks, ruined walls.

When rain beat down, swollen, angry
 As it falls the sky broke
A few stars emerging:
Could they be green?
Hesitant beams, small light.

Now moon rains down too,
And shadowing clouds at the ridge.
Round, full, comes the shine.

Half sunk inside the cove
The lone boat heaves, gasping.
The moon crests, lights each edge
The grey hill, the lustering flow.

Blue Harley

Headed for Lake Michigan
in my head I hear the waves.
A bar on every other corner
church spires casting shadows
ghosts in an old American Motors town.
Back alley aromas:
pasta sauce, tacos, kimchi, cumin
evoking neighborhood mysteries.

When a riot of light
spills out onto the street
draws me closer:
evanescence of electric blue.

All I can do
grab my camera
dive into cobalt air:
parked near the corner
classic chrome and leather
 the "H-D" etched into the seat.
Running lights full on
no rider in sight
clicks and laughter
from an open pool hall door.

I try to capture mesmery
in this rusty beer town.
Oh Blue Harley
who gets to hold you
between his thighs?

Main Street Marina

At the dock
waves lapping
sailboats bob—
lines assure
tension will hold
until winds blow stronger
waves roughen.

Rhythm of the sheets clanging
against the metal masts
fades against the foghorn's warning
a pulse syncopated
to the rounding pace of the north light.

A simple wooden skiff
slips its mooring
ebbs out
to wider starboard water
no hand to hold her

Drifting to the horizon
the boat becomes a point
while my breath
wanes with the outsweeping tide.

Nocturne for van Gogh in the *Saint-Re'my* Asylum

Iron barred windows
belie this yearning:
freedom is a brushstroked sky
nothing but the morning star
Venus, and a moon
turned crescent in his mind
as letters to his brother flowed
waving fields of wheat
real, and unreal
transmute to drowsing villagers
there, not there.

The cypress trees join earth to sky
"reminiscent of the north."
His fears:
"failure"—
endings transform:
"We take death to reach a star."

Yet ah, those stars—
spiraling nebulae of hope
joining with a moon
wrong for the season
but who questions
the aureole of imagination.

Field Station Reverie

Cedarburg

Aspen leaves fold
turning their backs to the wind:
shawl dancers swirling.

Late Monarch floats
testing wind and wings
waiting a sign to go.

Rustling behind me
four hooves leap the juniper
eye to eye: then gone.

The Secret

Navajo weavers
 embed a skip, a miss
a drop in the pattern—
reminder—
defiant imperfection
humbles the weaver and wearer.

Japanese potters emboss the broken
dark porcelain
it falls in shards
but the hands rework
with gilded lines
make the forsaken rare—
trace cracks
praised not hidden.

If I were the weaver, the potter,
all would be tangled threads
and gold.

Fear

Many poets fish
the lines must be
set
for casting, spinning
watching beds
for signs of spawn.

Fewer have walked
fall corn field ruts
in the small game dry spell
between bow and rifle seasons
found split hickories
and oozing black walnuts
fox dung
rusting farm gears
the spell of Canadas
in fog-laden air.

This fall
my boy found
a coyote family.
With pelts at forty a piece
would the young survive winter
without the mother?

I told him
pass up the shot
as you pass
the yearling buck

but I know
only the gameless hunter
knows the range
of the shot not taken.

December Quarry

I climb to see the sun
through the tangled trees.
Cliffs rise
high, narrow,
sheer faces
drop to water line.

Reflections below
break like shards
along the limestone faces.

Rain falls through the grey
turns to sleet
as I look up to the sound:
the haunt of geese lowers in.

Words slip through my brain
like the sand brought in.
Not a lake or pond,
it is a deep space filling.

How long did it take
for water to rise
this high,
for trees to fall,
quarry to water?

The geese know it well
as do I

come for refuge, escape
or forgetting.

The sounds from their throats
merge, and wind rises.
I watch them as they lower,
the solstice horizon
 I cannot see.
All is wingbeats on water.

Carol Lee Saffioti-Hughes, Ph.D., is a retired college professor *emerita* from the University of Wisconsin, Parkside, and a former librarian in a log cabin library in the north woods of Wisconsin. Some of her work has been translated into Chinese, and she has poetry published in England, Canada and the U.S. It has been anthologized in the *Root River Anthologies* and *Unsettling America* (Penguin Press). Her work appeared in journals including *The Greensboro Review, The Malahat Review, Poetry Hall, Poetry Quarterly, Awakenings, Rosebud, Moss Piglet*, and others. Her chapbook, *The Lost Italian and the Sound of Words* was published by Brighter Path Publishing. She is a member of the Wisconsin Fellowship of Poets, and of the Spectrum School of Art and Gallery in Racine. She also participates in zoom and live readings, including Woodland Pattern Wednesday Writers, the Root River Poets, and Zoom Poets. She lives in northern Wisconsin with her husband, much wild life, and hundreds of trees.

Several of the works included here have been published earlier: "From Where I Stand," Wisconsin Poets Calendar; "On Being Two Places at Once," *Rosebud*; "The Mothers," *Ekphrastic Review*; "The Bonsai Master," *Artery*.